What's in this book

This book belongs to

_____

多变的天气
The Unpredictable weather

学习内容 Contents

沟通 Communication

说说天气情况
Talk about weather conditions

说说衣着
Talk about clothes

生词 New words

★	天气	weather
★	太阳	sun
★	月亮	moon
★	下雨	to rain
★	下雪	to snow
★	帽子	cap, hat
★	鞋子	shoe
★	太	so
	晴天	sunny day
	刮风	(of wind) to blow
	围巾	scarf
	袜子	sock
	雨衣	raincoat
	雨伞	umbrella
	雪人	snowman

Grand Canyon

句式 Sentence patterns

太好了！
It is so good!

太可爱了！
It is so cute!

太冷了！
It is so cold!

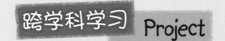

跨学科学习 Project

设计一个天气盘，并报道天气
Design a weather plate and report the weather

文化 Cultures

中国不同地区的不同气候
Climates in different parts of China

Get ready

1 Have you ever experienced changeable weather during your travels?

2 What are Ling Ling and her mother looking at?

3 What are Hao Hao and his father checking?

三月的最后一个星期，我们一家人
去大峡谷旅游。

第一天天气很好，太阳和月亮真好看。

第二天也是晴天，我们戴着帽子和围巾出去了。

路上突然刮风下雨，我们拿出雨衣和雨伞。

下雪
xià xuě

袜子
wà zi

鞋子
xié zi

然后下雪了，我们的鞋子和袜子都湿了。

但是我们很高兴。"太好了！下吧，
下吧！我们要堆雪人！"

Let's think

1 Recall the story and number the pictures. Write in Chinese.

2 Design funny weather signs to show the weather in the photos. Ask your friend to talk about the photos and match the signs to them.

这里真热！
人真多。

这里很冷。
天很黑。

New words

1 Learn the new words.

2 Listen to your teacher and point to the correct words above.

 1 Listen carefully. Circle the mistakes.

 2 Look at the pictures. Listen to the story a

1

2

3

昨天刮风下雨，今天早上下雪，现在有太阳了。

天气太冷了，我的帽子和围巾给它。

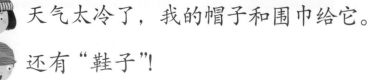 还有"鞋子"！

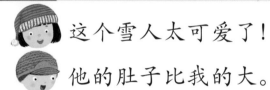

这个雪人太可爱了！

他的肚子比我的大。

你们看，月亮出来了，别玩了。

雪人雪人，明天见。

3 **Look and role-play with your friend.**

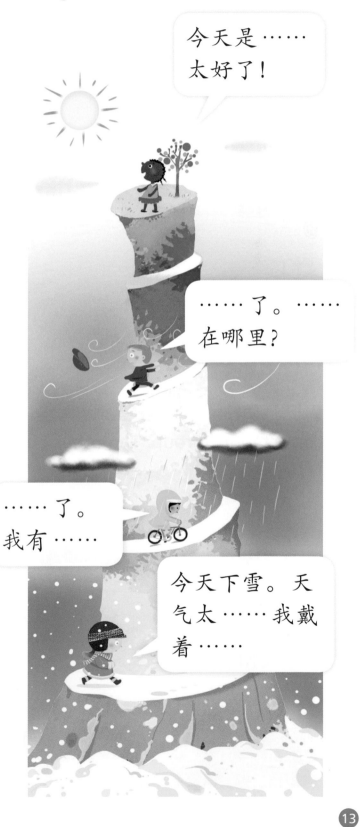

今天是……
太好了！

……了。……
在哪里？

……了。
我有……

今天下雪。天
气太……我戴
着……

Task

Draw yourself in your favourite and least favourite weather conditions and discuss with your friend.

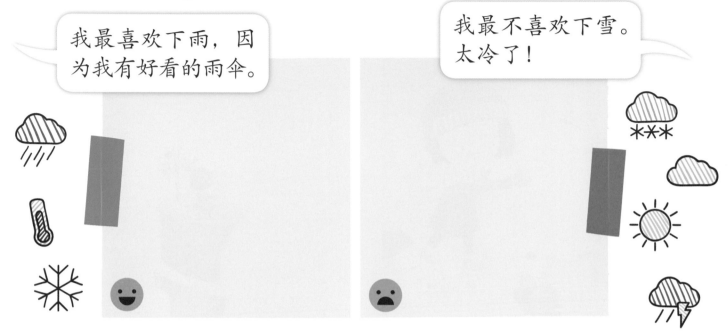

我最喜欢下雨，因为我有好看的雨伞。

我最不喜欢下雪。太冷了！

Game

Work with your friend and listen to your teacher. One of you point to the correct word group. The other point to the corresponding picture. See who is faster.

帽子、围巾

晴天、雨天

刮风、下雨

太阳、月亮

鞋子、袜子

雨衣、雨伞

Chant

🎧 05 Listen and say.

天气，天气，

可爱的天气。

白天有太阳，

晚上有月亮。

天气，天气，

多变的天气。

一会儿下雨，

一会儿天晴。

一会儿下雪，

一会儿刮风。

你拿雨伞和雨衣，

我拿围巾上学去。

生活用语 Daily expressions

天气真好。

The weather is great.

天气不太好。

The weather is not very good.

写一写 Write

1 Trace and write the characters.

一 ナ 大 太

了 阝 阝 阳 阳 阳

太	阳	太	阳
太	阳		

一 厂 厅 币 雨 雨 雨

雨	雨	雨	雨

2 Write and say.

_____圆圆的，真好看。

下___了。___真大。

3 Fill in the blanks with the correct words. Colour the stars using the same colours.

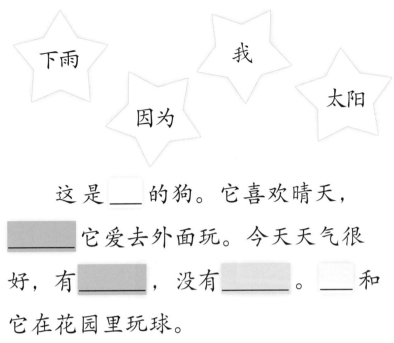

下雨

我

因为

太阳

这是 ___ 的狗。它喜欢晴天，_____ 它爱去外面玩。今天天气很好，有_____，没有_____。___ 和它在花园里玩球。

拼音输入法 Pinyin input

1 Listen to your teacher and compete with your friend. Who can finish typing the words on the sweets of the same colour faster?

阳　饭　雪　帽　笑　玩

今　月　子　胖　气　饿

圆　累　太　吃　早　鞋

天　画　亮　云　雨　家

红色的糖果。开始！

2 Challenge yourself. Can you type all of the words above in two minutes?

Cultures

The climate in China varies across the country because of its size. Can you match the descriptions to the photos? Write the letters and talk about the weather of each city.

太冷了！

今天是晴天。真热！

a	**b**	**c**	**d**
It has the coldest and longest winter among China's major cities.	It has a tropical climate and never snows during winter. There are typhoons in the summer.	It has four distinct seasons: a dry and windy spring, a hot and rainy summer, a cool and brief autumn and a cold winter.	It has a very mild climate. It is known as 'the City of Eternal Spring'.

1 What is the weather like this week in your city? Watch the weather report and draw the weather signs.

星期……	日	一	二	三	四	五	六	日
天气	☀							

2 Work with your friends. Make a weather plate and report the weather of this week.

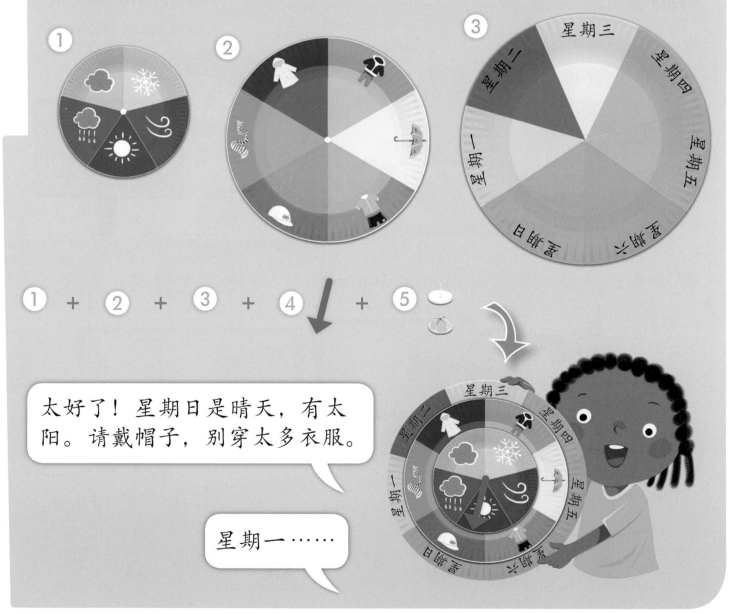

太好了！星期日是晴天，有太阳。请戴帽子，别穿太多衣服。

星期一……

温习 Checkpoint

1 Answer the snowmen's questions correctly to collect the medals. Which trophy can you get?

这是什么？
Answer in Chinese.

这是下雨还是下雪？
Answer in Chinese.

Start

Complete the sentence and read it aloud.

你喜欢运动吗？你累不累？ Answer in Chinese.

中文怎么说？

My shoes are too small.

今天天气太冷了。看，我有……和帽子。

你会看、会说吗？

Write the character.

今天天气好吗？

昨天刮风。今天是晴天。

我有 ☐ 伞。

今天有 ☐☐，太热了。

Finish

1–2 ○ : ★   3–5 ○ : ★   6–7 ○ : ★   8 ○ : 🏆

20

2 Work with your friend. Colour the stars and the chillies.

Words	说	读	写
天气	☆	☆	🌶
太阳	☆	☆	☆
月亮	☆	☆	🌶
下雨	☆	☆	☆
下雪	☆	☆	🌶
帽子	☆	☆	🌶
鞋子	☆	☆	🌶
太	☆	☆	☆
晴天	☆	🌶	🌶

Words and sentences	说	读	写
刮风	☆	🌶	🌶
围巾	☆	🌶	🌶
袜子	☆	🌶	🌶
雨衣	☆	☆	☆
雨伞	☆	🌶	🌶
雪人	☆	🌶	🌶
太好了!	☆	🌶	🌶
太可爱了!	☆	🌶	🌶
太冷了!	☆	🌶	🌶

Talk about weather conditions	☆
Talk about clothes	☆

3 What does your teacher say?

My teacher says ...

分享 Sharing

Words I remember

天气	tiān qì	weather
太阳	tài yáng	sun
月亮	yuè liang	moon
下雨	xià yǔ	to rain
下雪	xià xuě	to snow
帽子	mào zi	cap, hat
鞋子	xié zi	shoe
太	tài	so
晴天	qíng tiān	sunny day
刮风	guā fēng	(of wind) to blow
围巾	wéi jīn	scarf
袜子	wà zi	sock
雨衣	yǔ yī	raincoat
雨伞	yǔ sǎn	umbrella
雪人	xuě rén	snowman

Other words

大峡谷	dà xiá gǔ	the Grand Canyon
旅游	lǚ yóu	to travel
戴	dài	to wear
出去	chū qù	to go out
突然	tū rán	suddenly
拿出	ná chū	to take out
然后	rán hòu	then
湿	shī	wet
但是	dàn shì	but
下	xià	to fall
要	yào	to want to
堆	duī	to build

OXFORD
UNIVERSITY PRESS

Oxford University Press is a department of the University of Oxford.
It furthers the University's objective of excellence in research, scholarship,
and education by publishing worldwide. Oxford is a registered trade mark of
Oxford University Press in the UK and in certain other countries

Published in Hong Kong by
Oxford University Press (China) Limited
39th Floor, One Kowloon, 1 Wang Yuen Street, Kowloon Bay,
Hong Kong

© Oxford University Press (China) Limited 2017

The moral rights of the author have been asserted

First Edition published in 2017

Illustrated by Anne Lee, KK Ng and Wildman

Photographs for reproduction permitted by Dreamstime.com

China National Publications Import & Export (Group) Corporation is an authorized distributor of
Oxford Elementary Chinese.

Please contact content@cnpiec.com.cn or 86-10-65856782

ISBN: 9978-0-19-082253-8

10 9 8 7 6 5 4 3 2